Welcome to the "Enchanted Winter Wonderland Coloring Book." As you embark on this creative journey, may each stroke of color bring warmth and wonder to your heart.

For permission requests, write to the publisher: Dyson Independent Authors addressed
"Attention: Permissions Coordinator," at the address below:

Dyson Independent Authors
P.O. Box 17253
Jonesboro, AR 72403

First Edition: July 2024

Print ISBN: 978-1-962183-08-6

Printed in the United States

Imagine the crunch of snow beneath your feet, the sparkle of lights in the crisp night air, and the gentle whispers of winter's embrace. This book is your canvas to capture the enchantment of the season, to escape into a world of festive tranquility, and to create your own winter masterpiece. Happy coloring!

Step into a mesmerizing world where the magic of winter comes to life. "Enchanted Winter Wonderland Coloring Book" is filled with beautifully illustrated scenes of charming snow-covered villages, festive snow globes, and twinkling holiday decorations. Each page invites you to explore the joy and serenity of the season, bringing your artistic touch to a landscape of cozy homes, cheerful snowmen, and glowing Christmas trees.

www.ingramcontent.com/pod-product-compliance
Lightning Source LLC
Chambersburg PA
CBHW081005140626
46546CB00019B/3446